About the Book

A troop of mountain gorillas followed their big silverback leader. Moving toward the ridge for the night, they suddenly heard the crackling of branches nearby. Was this a friend or an enemy? The leader pursed his lips and hooted five times. He dashed wildly toward the sound, snatching up leaves and shrubs as he ran. He cupped his hands and beat his chest. Louder. Faster. The beating of his chest echoed through the forest, and his hooting blurred until it became a roar.

Here is the story of a newborn gorilla who lives deep in the Virunga Mountains of central Africa. Mikeno and the other young gorillas frolic together, playing follow-the-leader and tag. Mikeno scampers about, and likes to walk up and down his mother's back. The life cycle of the mountain gorilla is told in this Nature Biography, with paintings depicting the lush, exotic world it shares in the rain forest with antelopes, chimpanzees, black leopards, buffalo and elephants.

musanga

turaco

BIOGRAPHY OF A
MOUNTAIN GORILLA

by Lorle K. Harris   illustrated by Nancy V. A. Hansen

A Nature Biography

G.P. Putnam's Sons · New York

Text copyright © 1981 by Lorle K. Harris
Illustrations copyright © 1981 by Nancy V. A. Hansen.
All rights reserved. Published simultaneously in
Canada by General Publishing Co. Limited, Toronto.
Printed in the United States of America.
First impression.
Library of Congress Cataloging in Publication Data
Harris, Lorle K.
Biography of a mountain gorilla.
(A Nature biography)
Summary: Records the activities of a gorilla in central
Africa from his birth through his independence at the
age of four and a half to his formation
of a new troop after the age of nine.
1. Gorillas—Juvenile literature. [1. Gorillas]
I. Hansen, Nancy V.A.   II. Title.   III. Series: Nature
biography.
QL737.P96H37   599.88'46   81-5002   AACR2
ISBN 0-399-61144-4

For my children and grandchildren

Clouds drifted across the Virunga Mountains of central Africa. Now and again a peak showed through the mist, then was quickly hidden by the fog.

Rain drenched a mother gorilla huddled deep in the rain forest with her newly born infant.

Mikeno weighed only three pounds. He was less than half the size of a newborn human baby. Black fur covered his head like a cap, but the hair on his back, arms and legs was thin. The skin of his belly was brownish-pink and the brown skin of his hands and feet was dotted with pink.

At last the rain stopped and the mother gorilla rose to go back to her troop. She held Mikeno close to her chest with one arm as she tunneled her way through the underbrush, using the other arm like a third leg.

The gorillas were gathered together for
their midday rest. Adults stretched out on
the ground, or sat leaning against a tree or
log. Youngsters played follow-the-leader
and tag. Sometimes they scrambled over
the leader, who was the oldest and largest
of the gorillas. His back was silver-gray and

he stood nearly six feet tall and weighed three hundred pounds. His low forehead, with ridges that bulged over his eyes, and his heavy jaws made him look fierce. But the silverback let the young gorillas climb up on his huge chest and slide to the ground. Not until the play became too rough did he push them away.

The first to see the new infant was his four-year-old sister. She reached out to touch him, but their mother pushed her away gently. The little female coughed often because she was sick with pneumonia, a disease common during the rainy season.

Throughout the rest period, the gorillas glanced at the big silverback leader from time to time. About midafternoon, he rose and strutted off slowly. His stiff-legged gait was the sign the gorillas were waiting for, the signal to move on. Mikeno's mother rose.

One by one the gorillas followed the silverback, moving slowly on all fours. They turned their fingers under and walked on the knuckles of their hands with the soles of their feet flat on the ground. They pushed aside the ferns and moss that hung from the hagenia trees without breaking their stride. Sometimes Mikeno's mother

tugged at a lobelia stalk and stuffed it into her mouth.

After spending the day in the valley, the gorillas moved toward the ridge for the night. The gorillas had gone only a short way when the crackling of branches warned them that others were nearby. Were they friends or enemies?

The leader pursed his lips and hooted. *Hooo . . . Hooo . . . Hooo . . . Hooo . . . Hooo.* He dashed wildly toward the sound, snatching a handful of leaves from a nearby tree and stuffing it into his mouth. He pulled up shrub after shrub as he ran, only to throw them aside with an underhand motion. Again and again he repeated the five hoots. Then he cupped his hands and beat his chest. *Pok-pok-pok. Pok-pok-pok.* Louder. Faster. The other males joined the display.

The mother gorilla clasped Mikeno tightly and ran for cover in the woods. The sound of the chest beats echoed through the forest. The hooting blurred until it became a roar. From her hiding place Mikeno's mother saw the silverback rush madly ahead, kicking his feet, slapping and tearing at the foliage that blocked his way. Finally he thumped the ground with a slap of his hand and the display ended.

When the intruders were gone, the gorillas continued their journey to the ridge.

The leader stopped. *U-u-u*. *U-u-u*. He grunted repeatedly. It was time to bed down for the night.

The mother gorilla sat down under a tree. She held Mikeno firmly with one hand while she tore branches from a nearby bush with the other. She tucked the branches around herself in a ring. Then, lying on her side, she curled herself around Mikeno and fell asleep. Mikeno's sister slept nearby in a nest she built for herself. By the time the sun set, the gorillas were all asleep.

The band was a medium-sized troop of eleven animals. Each had his rank or place of importance in the group according to his age and sex. Next in line to the leader was a ten-year-old silverback. Two blackbacked males were next followed by three females. Because she had a new infant, Mikeno's mother was the top-ranking female. But the females didn't place as much importance on rank as the males. Two juveniles and two infants completed the troop.

The younger males and the females were only half as large as the silverbacks. Their fur was a shining blue-black and the black skin of their faces gleamed like polished leather. Their noses were flat, flaring out toward the nostrils. Each animal's nose was different, making it easy to tell them apart.

The leader signaled when it was time to rest, to feed, or to escape danger. The others obeyed. His leadership kept the group together and offered more protection than living alone.

The gorillas' range covered about fifteen
square miles. It overlapped the ranges of
other gorilla groups, but the groups usually
stayed apart. The rain forest provided so
much food that there was no need for the
band to stake out a territory of its own.

The gorillas slept late the next morning.
Clouds and fog still hid the sun at daybreak.
Nuzzling against his mother's breast, Mik-
eno found her nipple and nursed.

One by one the gorillas awakened. Some yawned and stretched and lay down again. Others sat in their nests and snacked on leaves. Mikeno's sister lay in her nest coughing so hard her body shook.

When the silverback rose, the others followed. They spread out behind him. The females and the younger animals stayed in the center of the troop while the black-backed males moved along the outer edges. The second silverback brought up the rear. This grouping offered the best protection to the mothers and their young.

But Mikeno's sister was too weak to keep up with the others. She lagged farther and farther behind until she was out of sight.

The gorillas were so busy looking for food that they didn't miss her. Nor did they hear her cries when a leopard carried her off.

The silverback led his troop from the lowland rain forest to the bamboo forest higher up the mountain. The bamboo sprouted during the rainy season and the tender young shoots were the gorillas' favorite food.

Mikeno's mother dug up the shoots hidden beneath the dead leaves on the ground. She stripped back the peel like a banana and ate the tasty white pith. She bit the larger shoots into sections, then split them with her incisor teeth to get at the pith.

It was quiet in the forest. Only an occasional belch, the snapping of a branch or the smacking of lips broke the silence.

At midmorning the silverback called out loud and clear. *Bu-bu-bu.* His call rose and fell in pitch. *Bu-bu-bu.* It was time to rest.

The rain still fell off and on. The apes sat hunched over and miserable letting the rain soak into their coats. The day-old Mikeno rested in his mother's lap. The silverback watched the mother gorilla study the infant's hands and feet and lick them. Then she groomed him, separating his hair with the index finger of one hand while she picked out bits of leaves with the fingers of the other hand.

Before long the rain stopped. Here and there the sun's rays streamed through a gap in the thick foliage. The gorillas moved over to the bright spots to sunbathe. They rolled on their backs, raising their arms above their heads to let the sun warm their chests.

Day after day the gorillas followed the same routine.

The gorilla baby grew fast, twice as fast as a human baby. When he was a month old he could grasp the fur on his mother's sides tightly enough to ride safely beneath her. He rested his head against her chest, hanging on with hands and feet as she walked or climbed a tree. Before he was two and a half months old he had cut his first teeth. The pink flecks on his hands and feet had disappeared and the skin had

turned dark brown, like that of his belly.

Mikeno not only looked different, he was bolder too. When he was three months old he could crawl and ride piggyback. He even walked up and down his mother's back sometimes if she was moving slowly enough. And he liked to sit, pulling leaves off the shrubs they passed and stuffing them into his mouth. A few weeks later, he rose on his hind legs and took his first step upright.

At last the rains that had poured steadily from September through December began to let up. January and February were fairly dry. In March the rain fell again, but not as heavily as in the fall. When the dry season finally came, lasting from June through August, the gorillas sunbathed often. Sometimes they lay in the sun for as long as two hours. Sweat gathered in beads on their faces and rolled down their chests.

By now Mikeno was seven months old and weighed eight pounds. He nursed occasionally, and would continue to do so for almost another year, but usually he ate the same food as his mother. He watched her pull down the long lobelia stalk with both hands and copied her. She bit hard into the stem and ripped away the tough outer layer with her teeth. He did the same. And when

she grunted with pleasure as she chewed
the juicy heart of the stalk, he imitated that
too.

One day Mikeno and his mother were feeding in a tree in which two young gorillas played. Suddenly one leapt on Mikeno's branch, jerking the limb violently. Mikeno tumbled to the ground screaming. He landed on the sharp point of a broken branch and cut a deep gash in his side.

His mother cried out and swung herself down beside him. She bent over to look at the wound. Mikeno whimpered as she picked bits of leaves out of the wound, then quieted down when she cradled him in her arms.

Another female, seeing Mikeno was hurt, came up to him. Puckering her lips, she touched his face gently. But when she tried to caress him again, Mikeno's mother pushed her away.

But the wound healed, and soon Mikeno was climbing trees again.

Feeding. Resting. Feeding. Sleeping. The routine of the gorillas' lives was much the same day after day and month after month. By the time Mikeno was a year old, his mother pushed him away gently if he acted too much like an infant. But she let him sit near her sometimes and occasionally she

groomed him. Mikeno and his mother stayed this way until she gave birth to an infant brother, when Mikeno was four and a half years old. Now his mother was too busy for him and he was completely on his own in the troop.

At five years Mikeno weighed a hundred and twenty pounds. He was strong and healthy and able to care for himself. By watching his mother he had learned which plants were good to eat and which he should avoid.

By now he knew the other animals that shared the rain forest: red duikers, small antelopes prized for their meat by the Batwa, a tribe of African pygmies; chimpanzees and black leopards that preyed on

young and sick gorillas. He seldom saw buffalo, because they grazed mostly at night. And like the other gorillas, he avoided the places where elephants had trampled down the vegetation.

Mikeno still romped with the other young gorillas sometimes. He liked to play tug-of-war, grabbing one end of a stick while another young gorilla pulled the other end. Other times he played follow-the-leader, or wrestled. If the game became too rough, Mikeno crouched down on his arms and legs, turning his back to his playmates. It was his way of saying, "I give up," and the game ended promptly.

But this didn't happen often because Mikeno was now one of the older juveniles. Several infants had been born into the troop since he was a baby.

One day when the gorillas were feeding the cry of a red duiker broke the quiet. *Pshi-Pshi.* Mikeno raised his head. Again the duiker cried out. *Pshi-Pshi.* Mikeno pulled a stalk of wild celery and munched. Suddenly the silverback roared. Mikeno looked up. He listened. A bough crashed. Branches crackled. The Batwa were coming!

Mikeno rose to his hind legs. He hooted and beat his chest. The other gorillas answered the danger signal, too. The blackbacks roared and beat their chests. Females and infants shrieked, adding to the din that echoed through the forest.

In his rush to escape, Mikeno plunged
into a duiker snare that hung from a tree.
The cord caught him around the shoulders.
The more he strained to break its grip, the
tighter it became. Mikeno roared in anger.
He pawed at the snare with his hands, but
the cord was so deeply imbedded in his
thick fur that he was unable to tear it. He
strained and strained, screaming with rage.
At last the cord snapped. Mikeno fled deep
into the forest.

When the forest grew still again, Mikeno looked for his band. By nightfall he had not yet seen any of the troop. He sat down beside a fallen log and tugged at the galium vines that covered it. He tucked the leafy branches around himself in a ring, curled up and fell asleep.

The next morning he followed a stream
that trickled down the mountain. He
avoided getting his feet wet by not crossing
to the other side until he found a log bridg-
ing the stream. All day he wandered looking for members of his troop, but he did
not find them until the next day.

During the years Mikeno was growing up, the size of the gorilla band changed from time to time. One of the blackbacks left to join another troop. Every three or four years each female gave birth to a new infant. And older gorillas, who seldom live more than twenty years in the wild, died. And so one day, the old leader disappeared.

When Mikeno was nine years old the fur on his back turned silver-gray. He was now twice as big as his mother. When he moved among the younger blackbacks they made way for him.

One day when the gorillas were feeding quietly the high-pitched scream of a juvenile startled Mikeno. He heard the swoosh and rattle of branches beaten to the ground and the tramp of feet and the cries of poachers drawing closer. Mikeno hooted. The silverback roared. The gorillas fled into the forest, but the poachers advanced steadily toward them.

Mikeno beat his chest and roared. He rose to his hind legs and dashed wildly into the underbrush. He snapped off branches as he ran, throwing them aside aimlessly with a flick of his wrist.

The hooting and screams of the gorillas filled the forest, but the poachers pushed on. They spread out in a half-circle to force the gorillas into the nets they had hung to trap them. Mikeno heard the gorillas screaming as they were beaten to death. He fled deeper into the forest.

Mikeno slept alone that night. And the next. He searched for days without finding any gorillas from his troop. He joined another gorilla band for a few days, then wandered off by himself. After several weeks he finally found his own band again.

One day when the troop was enjoying its midday rest, a pair of white-necked ravens circled overhead. They swooped down skimming over the gorillas' heads. The gorillas ducked. Mikeno roared. The ravens dived toward him, barely missing his head. Mikeno curled back his lips, showing his gums and teeth, brown with tartar. He roared again and again, alternately opening and shutting his mouth. The females screamed and dashed about in confusion while the ravens continued their teasing. At last they tired of their game and flew away.

Mikeno found a patch of sunlight and sat down to rest. A young female came over to him and clasped him around the waist. She pushed herself against him several times. Mikeno paid no attention at first, then suddenly turned and pulled her onto his lap and mated with her. They rested a while, sitting side by side. Then the female rose and stood behind him. He looked up at her and they stared at one another for several minutes. Then he pulled her into a sitting position and they mated again. Afterwards she rose and left.

Some days later Mikeno left the band and two young female gorillas left with him. He had started his own troop. The troop would grow as the females had infants and other lone males joined it, but Mikeno would remain the leader.

Author's Note

In prehistoric times the gorilla lived in a large area across western and central Africa. A long and severe drought destroyed the forest in the middle of the gorilla range. As a result, the gorillas were divided into two separate groups, living about six hundred fifty miles apart. They are now known as mountain and lowland gorillas.

Albert National Park, in Zaïre, was formed in 1925 to protect the gorillas. But this didn't stop people from moving into gorilla country. Cattlemen want their herds to graze in the park. Poachers hunt gorillas for their meat or to sell to zoos or medical research institutions. The poachers often kill all the adult animals in a troop to capture the young. But they don't know how to care for the young and they die too. The park rangers are so poorly paid that they often let poachers and cattlemen into the park in exchange for money.

Today there are probably only between five and fifteen thousand animals left. Unless they are better protected the gorillas will disappear from the earth.